Progressive JAZZ Studies

Etudes progressives de jazz
Fortschreitende Jazz-Etüden

for piano – level 1

pour piano – niveau facile
für Klavier – Grundstufe

John Kember

Contents/*Table*/Inhalt:

© 1995 by Faber Music Ltd
First published in 1995 by Faber Music Ltd
3 Queen Square London WC1N 3AU
Music set by Christopher Hinkins
Cover design by S & M Tucker
German translations by Dorothee Göbel
French translations by Brigitte Hagan
Printed in England by Caligraving Ltd

ISBN 0-571-51582-7

FABER *ff* MUSIC

Introduction

Jazz, rock and popular music use the same notation as the more established 'classical' forms, but are interpreted slightly differently: note values need not always be taken literally, but are used as a convenient way of indicating the rhythmic 'feel' of a pattern or phrase. Chords, broadly, function in the same way, but include various 'added notes' which give the harmony a jazz feel.

Jazz is as much a way of playing as a musical form, and so to play jazz well you need to develop:

- the ability to maintain a strict tempo
- total independence of the hands
- an understanding of and facility with chords
- an understanding of time patterns and jazz rhythms

These Progressive Jazz Studies aim to help you to:

- recognise and perform commonly-used time patterns with stylistic phrasing
- understand anticipation (syncopation) of both notes and chords and to perform it within a rigid tempo
- play against the beat in either hand, whether with single notes or chords
- form chords and recognise the sounds, textures and movements of notes within chords
- use either hand to build and maintain a chord sequence

By playing these short studies and pieces, you should build up a repertoire of styles and techniques, and also develop the confidence to extemporise in a variety of jazz styles.

Aspects of jazz rhythm

Pulse

The importance of keeping a regular pulse, and of the necessity to *count* cannot be over-emphasised. You must always know where the first beat of the bar is. This is particularly vital when improvising, where a similar sense of four- and eight-bar phrase lengths is also essential. Using a metronome when you practise can be very helpful in developing a good sense of rhythm.

Swing rhythm

In this book quavers/eighth notes should be played evenly as written. The 'swing' feel is indicated by

This will give a relaxed feel, particularly in right hand single note lines and melodies, and fits easily with triplets:

Anticipation

Moving a note or chord *forward* by half a beat.

Any beat can be anticipated, but the first and third beats (usually the strongest) are the most effective in giving a swing or jazz 'feel' to a simple melody or rhythm.

If the tied or anticipated note is accented, the phrasing becomes clearer and more stylistic, particularly if the preceding note is shortened.

If the anticipated note or chord is at the end of a phrase or is followed by a rest, it is better played staccato, or with an accented staccato.

The early studies in the book focus on anticipation of various beats, with melodic lines, chords and bass riffs (patterns).

Introduction

S'ils utilisent la même notation que les formes musicales plus "classiques", le jazz, le rock et la musique populaire sont interprétés d'une manière légèrement différente: les valeurs de notes ne sont pas toujours prises littéralement car elles représentent souvent une façon commode d'indiquer le caractère rythmique d'un motif ou d'une phrase. D'une manière générale, les accords fonctionnent de la même façon mais ils renferment diverses "notes ajoutées" qui donnent à l'harmonie le caractère du jazz.

Le jazz est autant une manière de jouer qu'une forme musicale, et pour bien en jouer il faut:

* tenir strictement le tempo
* posséder une indépendance totale des deux mains
* bien connaître et bien exécuter les accords, et enfin
* bien connaître les mesures et les rythmes de jazz.

Ces études progressives ont pour objectif d'aider l'interprète à:
* reconnaître et exécuter les mesures courantes avec un phrasé stylistique,
* maîtriser l'anticipation (syncope) des notes comme des accords et l'exécuter sur un tempo très strict,
* jouer à contretemps, à la main droite comme à la main gauche, les notes seules comme les accords,
* former des accords et reconnaître les sons, les textures et les mouvements des notes dans les accords,
* utiliser n'importe laquelle des deux mains pour former et tenir une série d'accords.

En jouant ces études et ces morceaux, aussi brefs les uns que les autres, l'interprète se constituera un répertoire de styles et de techniques, et il acquerra l'assurance nécessaire à improviser toute une variété de styles de jazz.

Aspects du rythme de jazz

Rythme

On ne saurait trop insister sur l'importance qu'il y a à tenir un rythme régulier et sur la nécessité de compter. Il faut toujours savoir où se trouve le premier temps de la mesure. C'est particulièrement important lorsqu'on improvise, de même que les longueurs de phrases de quatre et huit mesures. L'emploi d'un métronome lors de l'étude peut être très utile à l'acquisition d'un bon sens du rythme.

Rythme de swing

Dans le présent ouvrage, les croches doivent être exécutées de manière égale, comme indiqué. Le caractère de "swing" est marqué par

qui doit être joué

Cela comprend les notes liées et

D'où une impression de détente, notamment dans les lignes et les mélodies à notes seules de la main droite. Ce procédé permet aussi d'accommoder les triolets sans difficultés:

Anticipation

Il s'agit de déplacer une note ou un accord d'un demi-temps vers l'avant.

N'importe quel temps peut être anticipé mais les premier et troisième, qui sont généralement les plus forts, donnent mieux que nul autre le caractère du jazz ou du swing à un rythme ou une mélodie très simples.

devient

Si la note liée ou anticipée est accentuée, le phrasé devient plus clair et plus stylistique, surtout si la note précédente est raccourcie.

devient

Si la note anticipée ou l'accord anticipé se trouve à la fin d'une phrase ou s'ils sont suivis d'un soupir, mieux vaut les jouer staccato ou encore avec un staccato accentué.

ou

Les premières études du présent ouvrage traitent de l'anticipation de divers temps, avec lignes mélodiques, accords et riffs à la basse (motifs).

Einleitung

Jazz, Rock und Pop werden zwar auf dieselbe Weise wie die eher eingeführte 'klassische' Musik notiert, bei der Interpretation des notierten Textes gibt es aber kleine Unterschiede: die Notenwerte müssen nicht immer genau ausgezählt werden, sondern dienen eher als praktisches Hilfsmittel, um das rhythmische 'Feeling' einer melodischen Phrase oder eines rhythmischen 'Patterns' zu kennzeichnen. Die Harmonien werden insgesamt auf traditionelle Weise aufgebaut und eingesetzt, enthalten aber zusätzliche, akkordfremde Töne, die den typischen Jazzcharakter der jeweiligen Harmonie bewirken.

Jazz ist gleichermaßen eine bestimmte Art des Musizierens wie auch eine musikalische Form, so daß man verschiedene Fähigkeiten erwerben muß, um Jazz gut zu spielen:

- ein Tempo genau einhalten können,
- beide Hände völlig unabhängig voneinander führen,
- die Struktur der Harmonien kennen und im Umgang mit Akkorden versiert sein,
- die für den Jazz charakteristischen Rhythmen und 'Time patterns' (metrische Verhältnisse in unterschiedlichen Taktarten) kennen.

Die vorliegenden Jazz-Etüden in fortschreitender Schwierigkeit sollen dabei helfen:

- gebäuchliche 'Time patterns' zu erkennen und mit stilistisch passender Phrasierung zu spielen,
- die Antizipation (Vorwegnahme eines Tons oder Akkords, ergibt eine Synkope) von Noten und Akkorden zu verstehen und auch in schnellem Tempo auszuführen,
- in jeder der beiden Hände gegen die Zählzeit spielen zu können, sei es bei der Ausführung von Melodien oder Akkorden,
- Akkorde aufzubauen und die Klänge, Strukturen und Bewegungsrichtungen einzelner Töne im Akkord zu kennen,
- mit jeder der beiden Hände eine Akkordfolge aufzubauen und beizubehalten.

Durch das Erarbeiten der vorliegenden kurzen Etüden und Stücke erwirbt der Spieler ein Repertoire stilistischer Richtungen und Techniken und entwickelt außerdem genügend Selbstvertrauen, um in einer Vielzahl von Jazz-Stilen improvisieren zu können.

Grundlagen des Jazzrhythmus

Metrum

Die Bedeutung eines gleichmäßigen Metrums kann im Jazz gar nicht genügend betont werden, es *muß* gezählt werden. Der Spieler muß immer wissen, wo sich die erste Zählzeit im Takt befindet. Das ist bei der Improvisation besonders wichtig, wo man sich in ähnlicher Weise auch in vier- und achttaktigen Phrasen orientieren können muß. Durch das Üben mit einem Metronom läßt sich das Verständnis für den zugrundeliegenden Rhythmus stärken.

'Swing'

In der vorliegenden Ausgabe sollten Achtelnoten so gespielt werden, wie sie notiert sind. Der 'swing' wird durch die folgende Notation angedeutet ♩♪♩♪♩♪♩ auszuführen ist diese Notation so

Hierbei gibt es auch übergebundene Noten und

Eine solche Ausführung klingt locker und 'swingt', vor allem bei kleinen Phrasen und Melodielinien in der rechten Hand. Sie läßt sich gut mit Triolen kombinieren:

Antizipation

Bei der Antizipation wird eine Note oder ein ganzer Akkord eine halbe Zählzeit *vor* dem erwarteten Einsetzen gespielt.

Auf jedem Schlag im Takt kann antizipiert werden, am stärksten ist die Wirkung aber, wenn die erste und dritte Zählzeit im Takt (meist die starken, betonten Zählzeiten) antizipiert werden. Auf diese Weise erhalten eine einfache Melodie oder ein schlichter Rhythmus einen 'swingenden', jazzigen Charakter.

Wenn die übergebundene oder antizipierte Note einen Akzent erhält, wird die Phrasierung klarer und stilistisch für den Jazz typischer, vor allem dann, wenn die vorangehende Note verkürzt wird.

Wenn die antizipierte Note oder der antizipierte Akkord am Ende einer melodischen Phrase steht oder von einer Pause gefolgt wird, führt man den Ton oder den Akkord besser im Staccato oder gar mit einem akzentuierten Stakkato aus.

Die ersten Etüden in dieser Ausgabe beschäftigen sich mit der Antizipation bei verschiedenen Zählzeiten im Takt, mit melodischen Linien, Akkorden und ''Riffs' (vorgegebenen Mustern) in der linken Hand.

1 Bah-Ba-Doo Bah

Bah-Ba-Doo Bah · Bah-Ba-Doo Bah

Swing rhythm
Rhythme de swing
'Swing'- Rhythmus

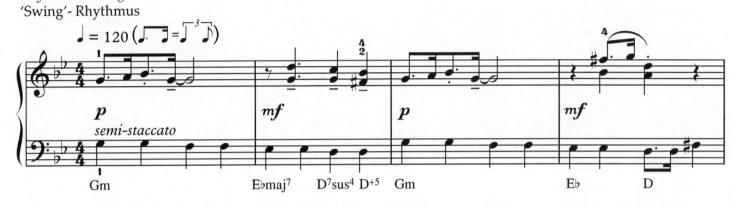

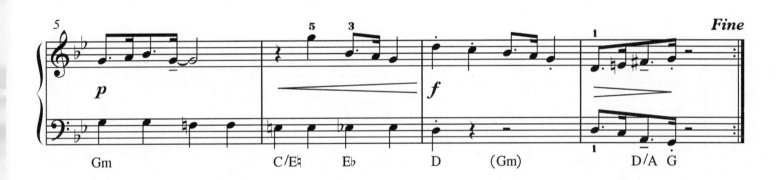

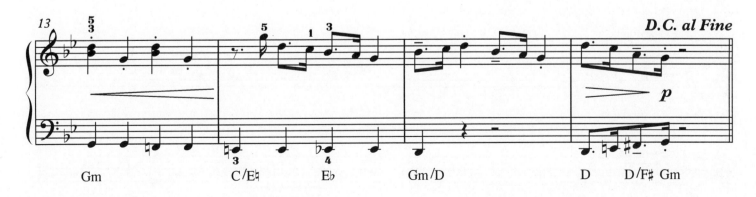

This music is copyright. Photocopying is illegal

2 Anticipation of Right Hand Chords

Anticipation des accords de la main droite · Antizipation von Akkorden in der rechten Hand

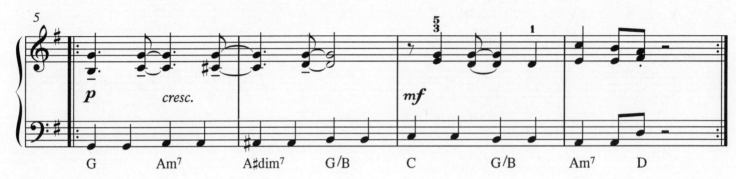

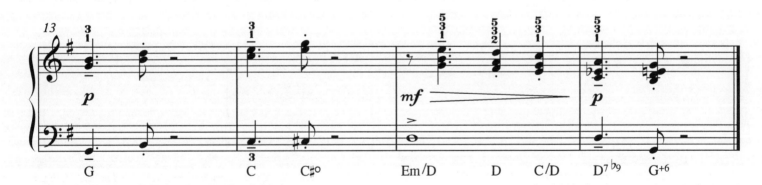

3 Anticipation of 1st Beat

Anticipation du 1er temps · Antizipation der ersten Zählzeit

4 Anticipation of 3rd Beat
Anticipation du 3è temps · Antizipation der dritten Zählzeit

Make sure that the chords are played *on* the beat and *after* the anticipated note
On veillera à jouer les accords sur le temps et après la note anticipée
Bitte darauf achten, daß die Akkorde *auf* den Schlag und *nach* der antizipierten Note gespielt werden

5 Anticipation within a Bass Line
Anticipation dans la ligne de basse · Antizipation innerhalb einer Bass-Linie

8

6 Chords: Anticipation of 4th and 1st beats; delayed 1st beat (common endings)
Accords: anticipation des 4è et 1er temps; 1er temps retardé (terminaisons habituelles)
Akkorde: Antizipation der vierten und ersten Zählzeiten; verzögerte erste Zählzeit (übliche Schlußwendungen)

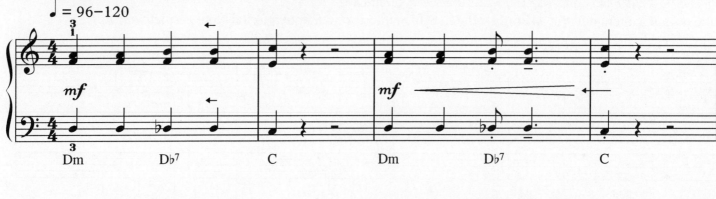

7 Anticipation of melody through to chords
Anticipation de la mélodie jusqu'aux accords · Antizipation, zunächst in der Melodie, dann bei Akkorden

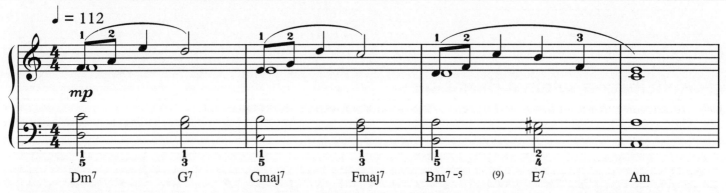

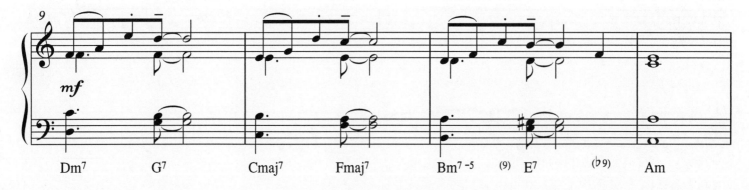

8 Right Hand developed from pentatonic scale

Main droite développée à partir de l'échelle pentatonique

Die Melodie der rechten Hand ist aus der pentatonischen Tonleiter abgeleitet

Em⁷ · Fmaj⁷ · Asus⁴/E · Am

Am⁷/G · Dm/F · G · Am · Am

Am⁷/G · Dm⁷/F · G · Am · Dm⁷/F · G

molto rall.

Am · Dm⁷ · G · Dm · Am

9 All White on the Night

Tous en Blanc Ce Soir-la · In dieser Nacht ist alles weiß

Bright 4 ♩ = 144

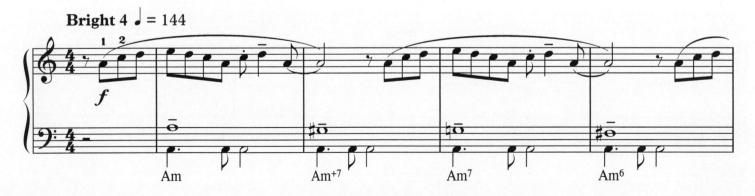

Am · Am⁺⁷ · Am⁷ · Am⁶

Chords

The common balance of chords is three notes in the right hand and single bass notes in the left hand, though this leaves little opportunity for melody, and normally chords need to be shared between the hands. Ideally, you should be able to play a chord sequence in either hand, and to incorporate a melody along with chords.

Study 10 shows a smooth progression of (mostly) 7th chords. Notice how the 7th *falls* in every case. The Left Hand Sequence (Study 11) leaves the right hand free to shape a melody or rhythmic pattern. Find the 7th in each 7th chord, and hear how it needs to fall by step to resolve.

Points to observe:
1. The smooth movement of notes from chord to chord.
2. The contrary movement between bass and moving parts of the chords (Study 10).
3. The movement of bass notes which give the sequence of 7ths.

Accords

Le schéma habituel d'accords est de trois notes à la main droite et d'une note à la basse. Mais cela ne laisse guère de place à la mélodie et les accords doivent généralement être partagés entre les deux mains. L'idéal serait de pouvoir jouer une série d'accords avec l'une ou l'autre des deux mains et de lui incorporer une mélodie ainsi que d'autres accords.

L'Etude 10 renferme une progression régulière d'accords de septième (pour la plupart). On remarquera que, dans chaque cas, la septième tombe. La Série pour main gauche (Etude 11) laisse la main droite libre de dessiner une mélodie ou un motif rythmique. Il suffira de chercher la septième de chaque accord de septième pour sentir qu'elle a besoin de tomber d'un degré pour se résoudre.

Points à observer:
1. *Le mouvement régulier des notes, d'accord en accord.*
2. *Le mouvement contraire entre la basse et les parties mobiles des accords (Etude 10).*
3. *Le mouvement des notes de basse qui donnent la série de septièmes.*

Akkorde

Üblicherweise gibt es bei akkordischem Satz drei Töne in der rechten Hand und eine einzelne Note in der linken Hand, obwohl bei dieser Verteilung auf die beiden Hände wenig Gelegenheit zu melodischer Gestaltung gegeben ist und Akkorde eigentlich zwischen den beiden Händen aufgeteilt werden sollten. Im Idealfall sollte der Spieler eine Akkordfolge in jeder der beiden Hände spielen und dabei gleichzeitig eine Melodielinie herausarbeiten können.

Etüde 10 zeigt eine Akkordfolge (vor allem Septakkorde). Man beachte, wie die Septe immer fällt. Die Akkordfolge in der linken Hand (Etüde 11) gibt der rechten Hand genügend Freiraum für eine Melodie oder ein rhythmisches Muster. Man suche die Septe in jedem der Septakkorde und achte darauf, wie sie zur Auflösung jeweils schrittweise nach unten geführt werden muß.

Wichtige Punkte, die nicht außer acht gelassen werden dürfen:
1. Eine gute Tonfortschreitung beim Wechsel von einem Akkord zum nächsten.
2. Die Gegenbewegung zwischen Basslinie und den nicht liegenbleibenden Tönen in der rechten Hand beim Wechsel von einer Harmonie zur nächsten (Etüde 10).
3. Die Bewegungsrichtung der Bassnoten, die zur Folge von Septakkorden führt.

10 Chords: Right Hand sequence
Accords: Série pour la main droite · Akkordfolge in der rechten Hand

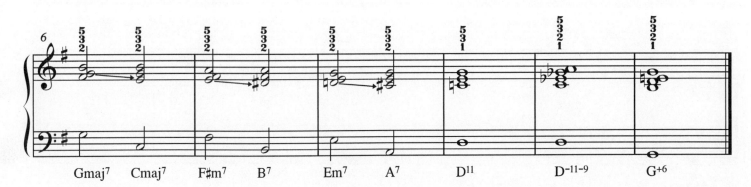

11 Chords: Left Hand sequence
Accords: Série pour la main gauche · Akkordfolge in der linken Hand

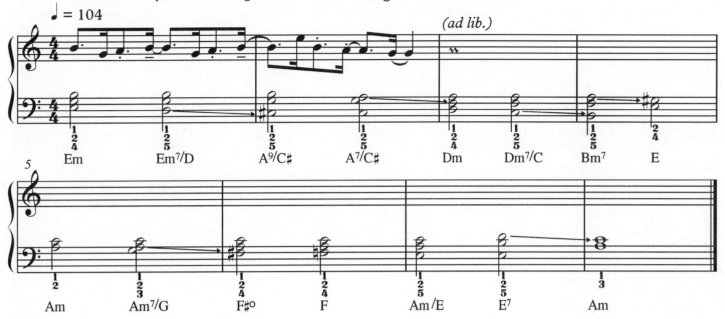

12 Anticipation of 4th beat
Anticipation du 4è temps · Antizipation der vierten Zählzeit

13 Chords: Right Hand against 'walking' Bass Line

Accords à la main droite et ligne de basse régulière · Akkorde rechts zu einem durchlaufenden Bass links

14 Serious Syncopation

Syncope sérieuse · Nachdrückliche Synkopen

15 So What!
Et puis après? · Na und!

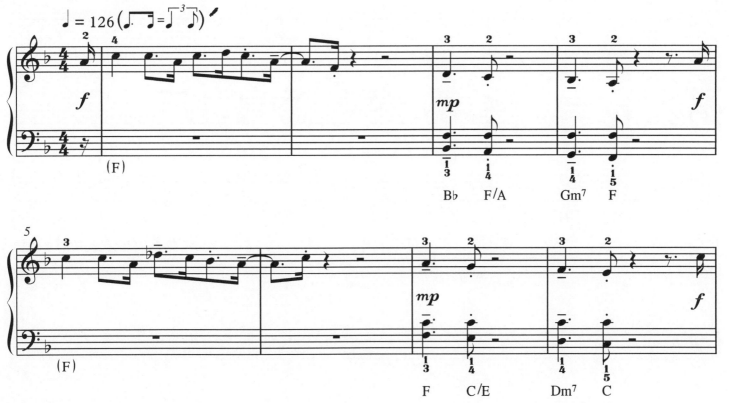

16 Step Time
Step Time · Step Time

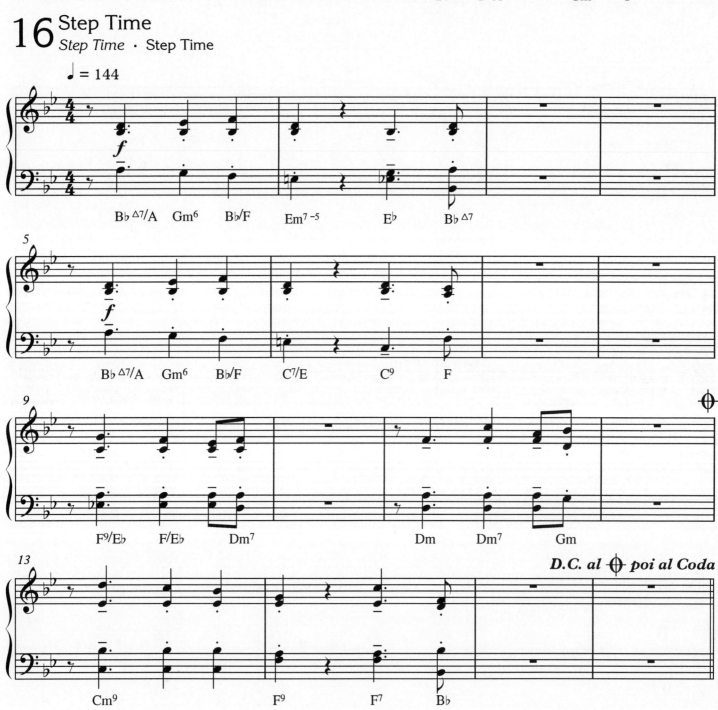

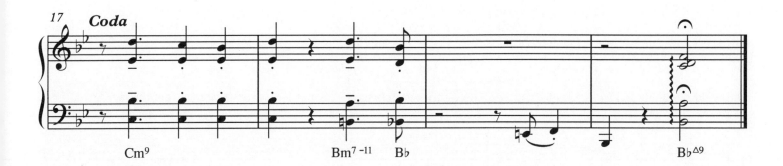

17 Window Shopping

Faisons les vitrines · Ein Schaufensterbummel

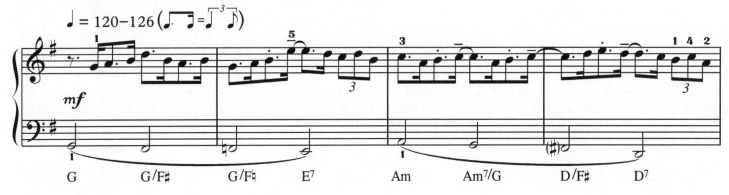

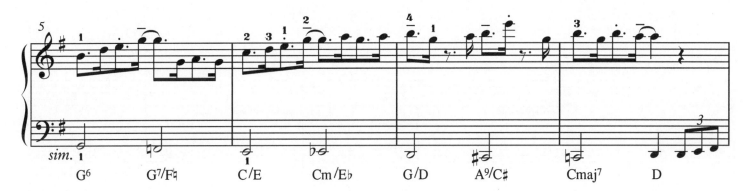

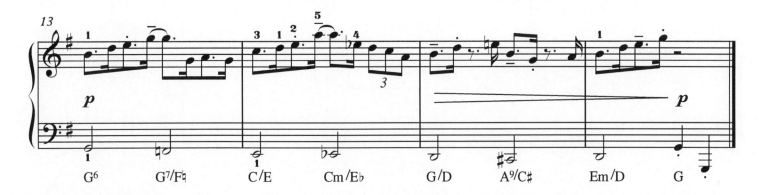

18 Naughty But Nice

Naughty But Nice · Unartig, aber reizend

The syncopated figure ♪♩ ♪ should be played as ♩♪♪♩♪, with the middle note staccato: ♪♩ ♪

La figure syncopée ♪♩ ♪ doit être jouée ♩♪♪♩♪, avec la note du milieu staccato: ♪♩ ♪

Die synkopierte Figur ♪♩ ♪ sollte so ♩♪♪♩♪ gespielt werden, wobei die mittlere Note *staccato* ausgeführt wird: ♪♩ ♪

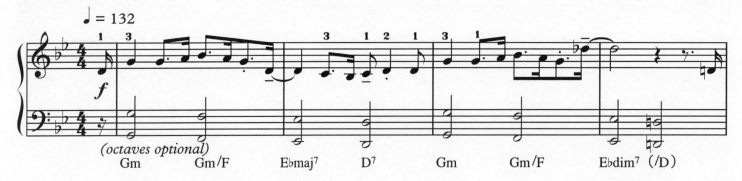

(octaves optional)
Gm   Gm/F   E♭maj⁷   D⁷   Gm   Gm/F   E♭dim⁷ (/D)

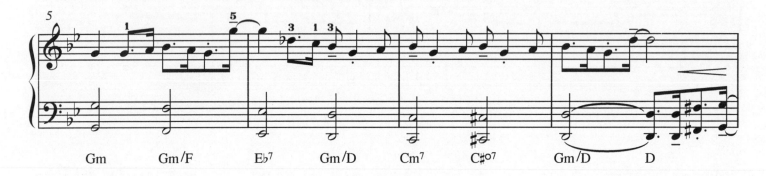

Gm   Gm/F   E♭⁷   Gm/D   Cm⁷   C♯°⁷   Gm/D   D

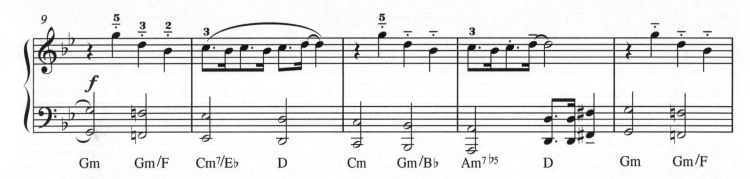

Gm   Gm/F   Cm⁷/E♭   D   Cm   Gm/B♭   Am⁷♭⁵   D   Gm   Gm/F

Cm/E♭   Cm   Gm/B♭   Cm⁷   D   Gm   Gm/F

E♭maj⁷   D⁷   Gm   Gm/F   E♭dim⁷   C⁷   D   D/F♯

19 Crushed Notes

Notes écrasées · Zerdrückte Noten

A feature of jazz piano, used as a form of accent: use them sparingly
Une caractéristique du piano de jazz utilisée sous la forme d'un accent: à n'employer que modérément
Beim Jazz Piano werden diese Klänge zur Akzentuierung benutzt. Nur sparsam einsetzen!

20 Open Spaces

Grands espaces · Offene Klangräume

Experiment with and vary the dynamics
Essayer et varier la dynamique
Experimentiere mit verschiedenen dynamischen Möglichkeiten!

21 Valse Semplice (waltz in jazz style)

Valse semplice (valse en style de jazz) · Valse semplice (Walzer im Jazz-Stil)

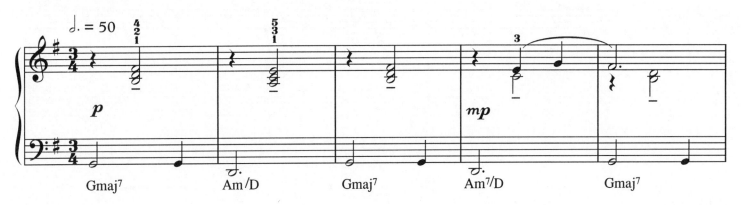

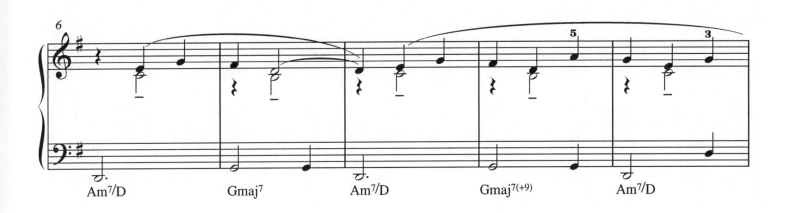

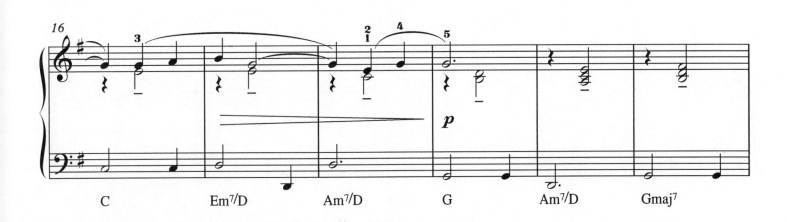

22 Jazz Waltz Study

Valse de jazz: étude · Etüde zum Jazz-Walzer

Get used to the rhythm before you begin:
On se familiarisera avec le rythme avant de commencer:
Probiere den Rhythmus aus, ehe Du beginnst:

Jazz waltz tempo ♩ = 160

23 Southern Belle
Belle du Sud · Southern Belle

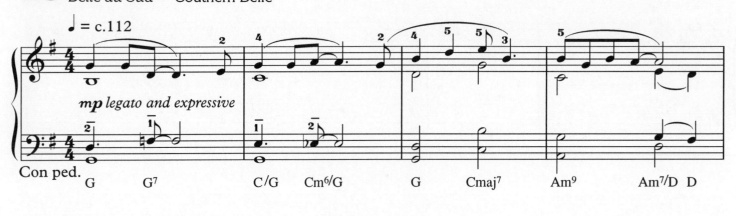

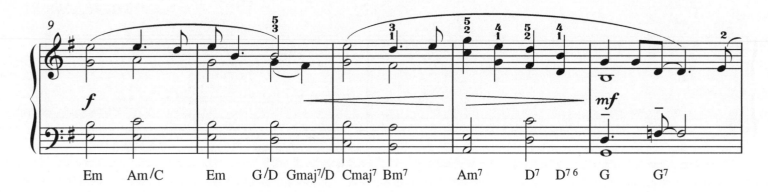

24 Romance
Romance · Romanze

Variations over left hand chord sequence
Variations sur une série d'accords à la main gauche
Variationen über eine Akkordfolge in der linken Hand

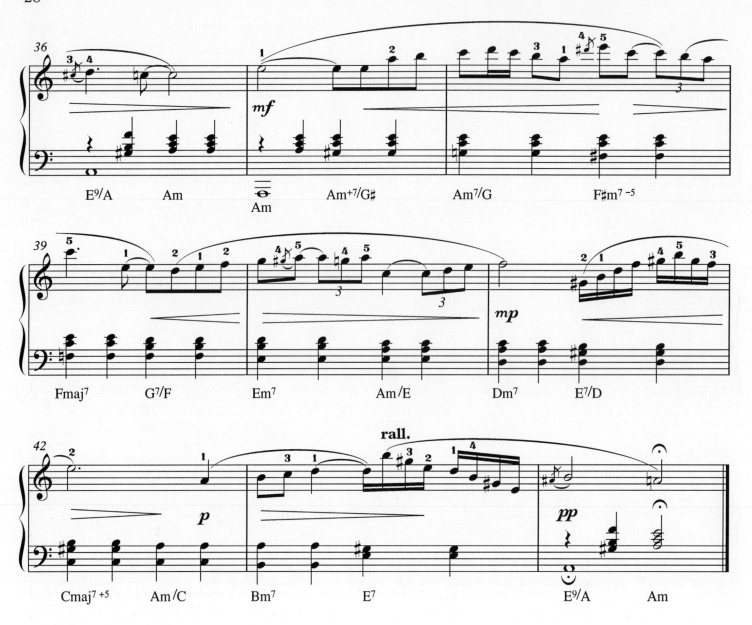

25 Feeling Good
On se sent bien · Es geht uns gut!

26 Small Talk
Bavardages · Plauderei

Swinging right hand chords
Accords de swing à la main droite
'Swingende' Akkorde in der rechten Hand

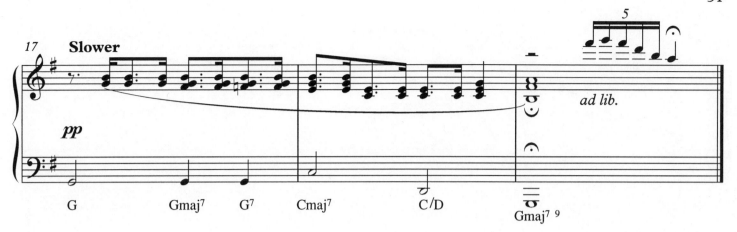

27 Night Life
Vie nocturne · Nachtleben

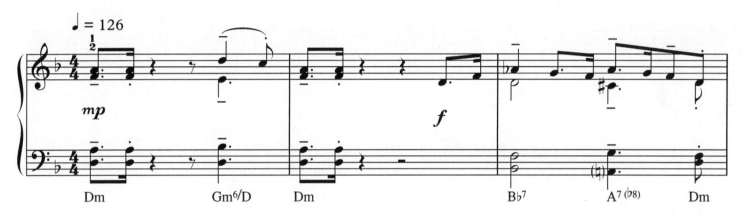

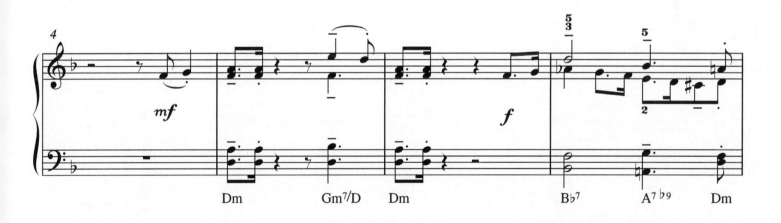

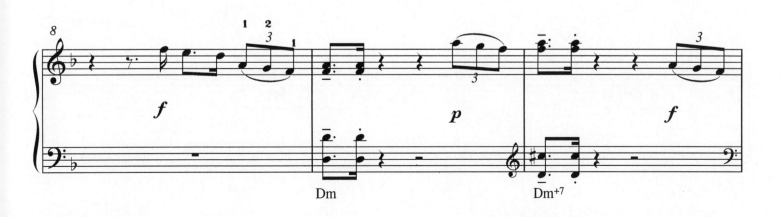